Original title:
The Frosted Dawn

Copyright © 2024 Swan Charm
All rights reserved.

Author: Kene Elistrand
ISBN HARDBACK: 978-9916-79-798-3
ISBN PAPERBACK: 978-9916-79-799-0
ISBN EBOOK: 978-9916-79-800-3

Frosted Horizons of Hope

In the morning light so pale,
Whispers of dreams ride the gale.
Snowflakes dance on a gentle breeze,
Painting the world with winter's tease.

Mountains wear their icy crowns,
Silhouettes against the towns.
Shadows stretch across the land,
Guiding hearts to take a stand.

Softly falls the silver dew,
Each drop a promise, pure and true.
Nature's canvas, bright and wide,
Holds the hope we cannot hide.

Underneath the frosty night,
Stars awaken, shining bright.
Their glimmers spark a quiet flame,
Whispering softly, calling your name.

Through the chill, we find our way,
Holding dreams that dance and sway.
With each step, let courage bloom,
In the frost, find warmth and room.

The Iced Veil Lifts Slowly

In the hush of dawn, whispers sigh,
The world beneath a blanket, shy.
Glistening wonders, silence reigns,
Nature's canvas, untouched gains.

Branches gleam with crystal tears,
Every corner, frost appears.
Shadows dance as sun ascends,
Magic weaves as daylight bends.

Morning's Frigid Brushstroke

With every breath, the winter bites,
Brushstrokes of white on starlit nights.
Frozen dreams in the pale light,
Awakening the day, soft and bright.

Pines stand tall in silent grace,
Wrapped in white, a soft embrace.
Footprints whisper on the ice,
Each step taken, a silent price.

Luminescence in Frost's Grip

Glistening fields, the dawn ignites,
Frosty jewels in morning's light.
Every blade, a diamond's might,
Nature dressed in purest white.

Shimmering crystals catch the sun,
Awake, the world has just begun.
In the chill, a spark ignites,
Life reborn in frosty sights.

Dawn Wrapped in a Silver Shroud

Misty whispers greet the day,
Silver hues in soft array.
Nature's breath, a frosty sigh,
Glimmers shine as shadows die.

Horizons stretch like painted dreams,
Ribbons of light in icy streams.
Wrapped in magic, the world unfolds,
As dawn reveals its silver golds.

Frosty Echoes and Radiant Colors

In twilight's grip, the frost does gleam,
A whisper soft, a fleeting dream.
Colors dance in icy air,
With every breath, a chilled despair.

Echoes ring from branches bare,
Nature's hush, a tranquil snare.
Shadows play on fields of white,
Painting realms in silver light.

The quiet strength of winter's hold,
Tales of warmth, forever told.
Beauty found in cold embrace,
A fleeting truth, a boundless space.

A Canvas of Ice and Light

Upon the pond, the glass reflects,
A world transformed, in pure aspects.
Frozen patterns softly spin,
A dance of light, where dreams begin.

The sun breaks through with tender grace,
Carving warmth in winter's face.
Colors bloom, a vibrant hue,
In icy realms, the heart feels new.

A canvas vast, with nature's art,
Crafted gently, a cold heart.
Each moment caught in dazzling sight,
In the chill, the world ignites.

Morning's Crystalline Melody

Awake to songs of frost and air,
A symphony of beauty rare.
Each note is crisp, a silver chime,
Made vibrant by the passing time.

Winds whisper through the frozen trees,
A serenade of winter's breeze.
Light cascades in diffused glow,
As crystalline dreams begin to flow.

The day unfolds in shimmers bright,
Embracing all with gentle light.
A melody that soothes the soul,
In every heart, it plays its role.

The Dazzling Whisper of Daybreak

In dawn's embrace, the shadows flee,
Golden rays, a warm decree.
Colors burst in bright display,
As night retreats, giving way.

Each morning brings a new design,
A canvas rich, where hopes align.
Soft whispers of the day aglow,
Nature's grace begins to flow.

Awakened dreams in sunlight's embrace,
A vibrant dance, a boundless space.
The world ignites with every hue,
In daybreak's breath, we start anew.

Morning's Crystal Lullaby

The sun peeks through the glass,
Bringing warmth to frosted trees.
Whispers of the dawn now pass,
Nature stirs with a gentle breeze.

Silhouettes of dreams take flight,
As birds begin their morning song.
Each note dances, pure delight,
In this world where we belong.

Beams of gold on silver dew,
A canvas of the day's embrace.
Painting skies in pastel hue,
In this ever-changing space.

With each moment, shadows play,
Transitioning from night to day.
Time suspends, then drifts away,
In morning's crystal lullaby.

Awakened by the Chill

The frost blankets the silent ground,
Every breath a misty sigh.
Whispers echo all around,
As sleepy stars begin to die.

The world is wrapped in a hush,
Where shadows stretch and dreams still lie.
Nature holds her breath in blush,
Underneath the winter sky.

Softly glowing, the moonlight fades,
As dawn approaches with a grace.
In this trance, the stillness wades,
Awakened by the chill's embrace.

A shiver dances down my spine,
Yet warmth ignites within my heart.
The day unfolds with new design,
As light and shadow play their part.

Celestial Frost Lifting

Morning light begins to rise,
Chasing shadows from the night.
Celestial frost, a sweet surprise,
Sparkles gently in the light.

Each crystal breaks with dawn's first kiss,
A fleeting moment, then it's gone.
Nature's breath, a tranquil bliss,
As day reveals, we carry on.

The whispering winds tell tales anew,
Of what is lost and what remains.
Each petal touched by morning dew,
Rejoices in the sun's refrains.

With every ray, a promise made,
Of warmth and life, a fresh embrace.
The frost retreats, no longer stayed,
Inviting us to join the race.

Moments in Ice and Light

In quiet stillness, hearts take flight,
Moments frozen, pure and bright.
Delicate as the morning's sigh,
Wrapped in warmth from the frigid sky.

The world a canvas, painted clear,
Each crystal holds a hidden spark.
Time stands still, yet draws us near,
In every corner, light and dark.

Reflections shimmer on the stream,
Where shadows dance with soft delight.
As day unfolds, we find the dream,
In moments caught in ice and light.

Nature whispers secrets bold,
A tapestry of tales untold.
Embraced in warmth, in heart and soul,
We find our way, we become whole.

Frosted Whispers in the Breeze

The trees stand still, a silent grace,
Frosted whispers dance in space.
Gentle breezes softly sigh,
As morning light begins to fly.

Each breath of chill a sweet embrace,
Nature's canvas, white and lace.
The world awakes, so fresh, so new,
In the hush of dawn's soft hue.

A fleeting moment, crisp and clear,
Magic lingers, ever near.
Echoes of winter's soft caress,
In the quiet, we find our rest.

Dewdrops sparkle, diamonds found,
Whispers of frost, a soothing sound.
In this beauty, hearts align,
Lost in wonder, pure divine.

A Shimmering Prelude

Twilight dances on the edge,
A shimmering light, a soft pledge.
Stars awake in velvet skies,
Whispers of night, where magic flies.

The first breath of night, so sweet,
A symphony where shadows meet.
Moonlight spills on silken streams,
Illuminating our sweetest dreams.

Each moment hangs, a fragile thread,
Bathed in silver, softly spread.
The heart beats with a rhythmic tune,
In the cradle of the moon.

A prelude to the dreams we weave,
Underneath the stars, we believe.
In the stillness, hopes ignite,
As the world slips into night.

The Soft Kiss of Ice on Grass

Morning breaks with tender light,
A soft kiss warms the chilled night.
Ice retreats, the world awakes,
Gentle whispers, the daylight makes.

Each blade of grass wears diamond tears,
Reflecting beauty through the years.
Nature's touch, a loving muse,
In the sunlight, warmth diffuse.

Frosty remnants start to fade,
A canvas where new tales are laid.
The earth exhales, a breath of spring,
Awakening life, a tender fling.

Beneath the ice, soft roots take hold,
Stories of life and love retold.
In the quiet, growth begins,
As warmth returns, the heart now spins.

Crystal Shadows in Morning's Glow

Morning light spills through the trees,
Casting shadows with the breeze.
Crystal drops of dew adorn,
Each petal shines, a day reborn.

Golden rays embrace the earth,
Whispers of new life, a birth.
In this soft, ethereal show,
Nature glistens, a gentle glow.

Shadows dance upon the ground,
In their waltz, a magic found.
Every leaf, a story told,
In hues of jade and softest gold.

The world awakens, fresh and bright,
Embracing warmth, chasing night.
With open arms, we greet the day,
In morning's glow, we find our way.

Whispers of Morning Mist

In the quiet dawn's embrace,
Soft whispers fill the air,
Dewdrops cling to blades of grass,
Nature's breath, a gentle prayer.

Colors bloom in muted tones,
As sunlight tips the trees,
Shadows dance on velvet hills,
Carried by the waking breeze.

The world awakens, slow and sweet,
Each heartbeat, a tender song,
Birds set forth their morning calls,
In a symphony that feels so strong.

Misty veils begin to lift,
Revealing paths of gold,
A canvas fresh, unmarred by time,
Where stories silently unfold.

Whispers blend with every sigh,
Promises of a brand new day,
In the stillness, hope takes flight,
Guiding us along the way.

Icy Veils of Awakening

Through the frost, a blanket lies,
A serene and shimmering sight,
Icy veils drape every branch,
Glinting softly in the light.

Branches bow with silver weight,
Whispers of the silent cold,
Nature's art, so delicately,
In the stillness, tales unfold.

Each breath becomes a frozen cloud,
As the world holds its breath near,
Crystals dance on shallow streams,
In this moment, everything is clear.

With each step, a crunch of frost,
Echoes of a winter's dream,
Awake to life, yet wrapped in sleep,
The beauty holds us in its gleam.

Icy veils, a gentle shroud,
Enfolding earth in frozen grace,
As daybreak paints the scene anew,
With colors soft, in time and space.

Crystals on the Horizon

Glittering shards greet the eye,
As dawn unfolds her gaze,
Crystals sparkle on the waves,
Reflecting soft, golden rays.

The horizon meets the sea,
Where dreams break with the tide,
Every crest a whispered promise,
In each swell, joy does abide.

Seagulls dance in morning air,
Painting patterns bold and bright,
While the ocean hums a tune,
A melody of pure delight.

Waves, like laughter, rise and fall,
Glistening with the morning sun,
Each moment, a fleeting grace,
In the rhythm of the run.

Crystals gleam, the world awakes,
A tapestry spun with care,
In the light of new beginnings,
A symphony beyond compare.

Glacial Light at Sunrise

Underneath the glacial sky,
The sun begins to rise,
A tapestry of icy hues,
Greeting morning with surprise.

Frigid air holds quiet dreams,
As shadows slowly fade,
The world adorned in frosty gems,
In this tranquil masquerade.

Mountains crowned with glistening crowns,
Stand sentinel and proud,
While the light spills over peaks,
In whispers soft yet loud.

Each ray, a brush of warmth and gold,
Chasing night away,
Awakening the sleeping earth,
In the dawn's sweet ballet.

Glacial light, a calming peace,
Enveloping the land with grace,
A moment where all aligns,
In this sacred, quiet space.

Ethereal Mornings in Winter Hues

Soft whispers of the chill air,
Blankets of frost everywhere.
A gentle glow begins to rise,
Underneath pale, silver skies.

Footsteps crunch in morning's light,
Shadows stretch, a fleeting sight.
Nature wrapped in icy glow,
As the world begins to slow.

A tranquil hush embraces trees,
While breath turns to mist with ease.
The sun peeks out, shy and bright,
Painting dawn in pure delight.

In this realm, serene and deep,
Promises of dreams we keep.
Ethereal moments take their flight,
In the magic of winter's light.

A Canvas of Icy Dreams

Whispers weave through frosted air,
A canvas pure, beyond compare.
Brush strokes of winter's embrace,
Create a calm, enchanting space.

Each tree a sculpture, standing tall,
Nature's artistry, captivating all.
Icicles dangling, glimmering bright,
Reflecting the dawn's soft light.

Rivers sleep beneath thick ice,
Time stands still, a frozen slice.
Every flake, a tale to share,
Drifting gently, light as air.

A world adorned in white and blue,
With every breath, a promise new.
Dreams awaken, soft and clear,
In this winter, magic draws near.

Snowflakes Dance with the Dawn

Snowflakes twirl in graceful flight,
As dawn awakens, pure and bright.
Each one unique, a tale untold,
A soft ballet, a sight to behold.

Silver sparkles catch the sun,
As winter dances, just begun.
The world adorned in crystalline,
Whispers of peace, so divine.

The silence sings a soothing tune,
Beneath the watchful, glowing moon.
Footprints left on crystal ground,
In this beauty, joy is found.

As shadows play and colors bloom,
A canvas stretched across the gloom.
Snowflakes dance with glee today,
In the dawn's bright, warm array.

The Dawn's Glacial Palette

In the hush of morning's breath,
Nature whispers tales of death.
Yet life stirs under ice so sly,
As the dawn paints the distant sky.

Pastels mingle in frigid air,
A glacial palette, rich and rare.
Lavender clouds, pinks rising high,
Soft hues that breathe, and gently sigh.

Beneath the frost, the earth still sleeps,
While winter's secret carefully keeps.
Every sunrise brings chance anew,
In the blend of every hue.

The world transformed, an artist's dream,
Where silence reigns, and spirit gleams.
The dawn awakens frosty glades,
In winter's trust, as light cascades.

Sunlit Crystals Unfold

Beneath the dawn's soft gleam,
Crystals shimmer, dreams take flight.
Each glint a fleeting theme,
In morning's gentle light.

Nature's jewels find their place,
Reflections dance in the air.
Graceful forms, a fleeting grace,
Every corner holds a flare.

The dew drops sparkle bright,
Whispers of a brand new day.
A canvas kissed by light,
Where shadows waltz and play.

In this serene embrace,
Sunlit magic unfolds wide.
A world wrapped in lace,
As darkness sets aside.

With every golden ray,
The heart hums a sweet tune.
Where joy and hope convey,
A love for the warm June.

Fragments of Light on Frozen Fields

Frosty echoes in the breeze,
Shimmer across the frozen land.
Frozen fields, a quiet tease,
Where stillness makes a stand.

Glints of sunlight break the dawn,
A million stars upon the ground.
Winter's grace, like a fawn,
In silence, beauty found.

Every flake a fleeting kiss,
Nature's art, both bold and bright.
A moment wrapped in bliss,
As day defeats the night.

Tracks of critters, soft and light,
Tell stories of a world awake.
Crisp air, pure and right,
In every breath we take.

Whispers of the icy air,
Fragments dance as if in glee.
Nature's charm is everywhere,
A frozen tapestry.

An Icy Serenade of Colors

Crystal notes on winter's breath,
An icy song, serene delight.
Harmony woven till death,
In colors pure and bright.

Blues and whites in frosted grace,
Swaying softly with the trees.
Nature's canvas in its place,
A symphony in the breeze.

With each hue a gentle tune,
Melodies that softly call.
Underneath the watchful moon,
Winter's beauty, a soft thrall.

Each flake a note, a sweet refrain,
Falling softly, so divine.
In the hush, a soft sustain,
Painting love with every line.

An exquisite dance unfolds,
In the quiet of the night.
The icy serenade molds,
A moment wrapped in light.

Frosty Boughs and Sunkissed Skies

Frosty boughs hold secrets vast,
Glimmers touch each brittle leaf.
Whispers of the winter past,
A moment caught, sweet relief.

Sunkissed skies above the trees,
Paint strokes of gold and amber.
Dancing lightly on the breeze,
A warm embrace, a tender slumber.

The world glows in twilight's glow,
Colors blend with soft delight.
As day bids a soft goodbye,
The night hums a lullaby.

From frost to warmth, the cycles flow,
Nature's art, sincere and true.
In this dance, we gently row,
Embracing every hue.

For every moment holds a spark,
A memory wrapped in time.
In the light, where shadows arc,
Life's beauty is a rhyme.

Aurora of the Glazed Morning

The dawn cracks through the haze,
Its light a gentle blaze.
Whispers dance upon the breeze,
Awakening the trees.

Colors blend in soft delight,
Painting skies with purest light.
In the stillness, shadows play,
As night gives way to day.

Warmth unfurls beneath the sun,
Embracing all, we've just begun.
Each moment sparkles, pure and bright,
A promise born of morning light.

Nature sings a joyous tune,
Lifted by the rising moon.
In this tranquil hour of grace,
Life begins to find its place.

So let us cherish every glow,
In the dawn, our spirits flow.
With each step, we find our way,
Transforming dreams in golden sway.

Ethereal Hues of Ice

In frosted air, colors gleam,
A shimmering and fragile dream.
Crystals dance upon the ground,
In silence, beauty's whisper found.

Glistening under winter's reign,
Nature sways in gentle pain.
Each shard reflects a story told,
Of ancient times, of ages old.

Cascading droplets on the trees,
Catch the light with graceful ease.
The chill embraces every hue,
A canvas vast, with strokes so true.

Winds weave through the moonlit night,
Guiding souls to sheer delight.
In this realm of icy sighs,
Magic lingers, never dies.

So take a breath, embrace the chill,
Let your heart with wonder fill.
In ice's grasp, we find our peace,
As colors blend and never cease.

Crystal Dawn's Embrace

Morning breaks with soft caress,
Awakening the world in finesse.
Beneath the sky, a tender glow,
Nature whispers, rivers flow.

Glistening dewdrops, pearls aligned,
Each one holding dreams unconfined.
The air is fresh, alive with grace,
As shadows slowly find their place.

Birds take flight on angel's wings,
Heralding all that morning brings.
In hues of rose and amber light,
The day unfolds, a pure delight.

Through leaves once bound by darkest night,
A symphony of warmth takes flight.
Every heartbeat, every sigh,
Echoes love beneath the sky.

So hold this moment, breathe it in,
As daylight's dance begins to spin.
In crystal dawn, our hopes embraced,
Together, we find our sacred place.

Shard-like Glimmers of Day

Sunrise spills its liquid gold,
Casting dreams that dare be bold.
Through the veil, the shadows break,
With every breath, a chance we take.

Glimmers catch the morning dew,
Reflecting joy in every hue.
Each ray a promise, pure and bright,
Illuminating hearts with light.

Whispers of the waking trees,
Rustle softly in the breeze.
Nature sings a vibrant song,
In this moment, we belong.

Shards of brilliance fill the air,
Weaving magic everywhere.
Each instant glows, a fleeting spark,
Guiding dreams from light to dark.

So share this dance with every dawn,
In every step, our spirits drawn.
Hold tight the glimmers, let them stay,
In shard-like moments of the day.

The Artistry of Frozen Glimmers

In silent hues, the world lies still,
Each flake a story, nature's quill.
A tapestry woven with care,
Artistry glimmers in the crisp air.

Branches adorned with icy lace,
Shimmering jewels in a cold embrace.
Beneath the moon's soft, radiant light,
Frozen glimmers dance through the night.

The earth dressed in a sparkling gown,
A masterpiece, the winter's crown.
Footprints traced upon the snow,
Stories whispered, soft and slow.

Around each corner, wonder waits,
Nature's wonder behind the gates.
In every shimmer shines a tale,
Of seasons past, of dreams set sail.

As morning breaks with gentle grace,
The frosted air, a warm embrace.
In this artistry, we find our place,
Frozen glimmers, nature's face.

Serenity in Frosted Beginnings

Morning awakens with tender light,
A world transformed, pure and bright.
Frosted whispers greet the dawn,
In serenity, a new day's born.

Trees stand tall, their branches bare,
Adorned with crystals, beyond compare.
Each breath a cloud of silvery mist,
In this quiet, nothing's missed.

The silence sings, a tranquil song,
In frosted beauty, we all belong.
Birds take flight in shimmering air,
Their wings trace patterns, light as prayer.

With every step, the earth may crack,
Yet joy is found in looking back.
In frosted beginnings, hope takes root,
In winter's chill, life's absolute.

As moments pass, the sun will rise,
Painting gold upon the skies.
Serenity wrapped in white embrace,
Frosted beginnings, a sacred space.

Glistening Echoes of Morning

In dawn's embrace, the world awakes,
Glistening echoes, the heart it takes.
Every blade of grass adorned with frost,
In shimmering silence, no moment's lost.

Treetops shimmer with jeweled light,
Transforming shadows into bright.
Whispers of beauty in the chill,
Nature's canvas, quiet yet still.

Beneath the sky, vast and wide,
The sun creeps up, a golden tide.
With every glow, new dreams arise,
In glistening echoes, the spirit flies.

As time unveils its gentle hand,
Frosty gems across the land.
Each echo sings a tale of old,
Of warmth and wonders yet untold.

Moments linger in the sweet repose,
Where magic dances, and love bestows.
Glistening echoes fill the day,
In morning's light, we find our way.

Frost's Lullaby at Dawn

Hush now, the world is wrapped in white,
Frost's lullaby sings soft and light.
Underneath the stars' fading glow,
Peaceful dreams swirl, gentle and slow.

The earth dons a delicate veil,
In winter's embrace, stories prevail.
Muffled whispers through the trees,
Nature's song carried on the breeze.

Each breath taken, frosted and sweet,
In this moment, life feels complete.
A lullaby tender, sweet refrain,
In this frosty realm, joy remains.

Awakening to the crisp delight,
The dawn breaks with a hue so bright.
Stirring gently, all things alive,
In frost's embrace, spirits thrive.

Frost's lullaby, a tender call,
Inviting peace to one and all.
In morning's warmth, our hearts will sing,
For in each dawn, new hope we bring.

The Chill of New Beginnings

A breath of winter's sigh,
Awakens the dormant earth.
Soft flakes fall from pale skies,
Blanketing all in mirth.

Fresh starts in every flake,
Whispers of dreams untold.
Beneath the icy wake,
Life stirs, brave and bold.

Branches bow in silence,
Crystals dance on the breeze.
In the gentle cadence,
Hope blooms among the trees.

Chill winds weave through the night,
Carrying stories near.
Under the silver light,
A new world draws us here.

The dawn breaks cold and bright,
With promises to keep.
In the stillness, delight,
As nature drifts to sleep.

Twilight's Frosted Embrace

Twilight drapes its cloak,
A shroud of frosted dreams.
Where shadows softly spoke,
And the world shimmers and gleams.

Stars blink their gentle light,
On landscapes kissed by frost.
Nature whispers goodnight,
In this moment, not lost.

The crescent moon hangs low,
Dancing with twilight's mist.
Through fields of shimmering snow,
Each moment feels like bliss.

Frozen echoes of joy,
In the stillness, we find peace.
Ceaseless wonders deploy,
In the night's sweet release.

In this frigid embrace,
Hearts warm beneath the sky.
Together we find our place,
Where the whispers of dreams lie.

Where Ice Meets Light

At the edge of the dawn,
Where ice meets golden rays.
Nature blushes and fawns,
In this mystical phase.

Crystals catch sunlight's kiss,
Transforming the morning dew.
In this moment of bliss,
Life begins fresh and new.

Frosty breath on the air,
Carried on gentle winds.
In this dance, hearts laid bare,
As the silence rescinds.

Glimmers of hope arise,
In the warmth of the sun.
Where the chill slowly dies,
And the world comes undone.

Joy found in every gleam,
As shadows fade away.
In this delicate dream,
We greet another day.

The Birth of a Crystal Dawn

From the darkness, a spark,
Unfurls to greet the morn.
In the silence, a mark,
New beginnings are born.

Frost clings to every leaf,
Silver threads in the light.
A whisper of belief,
As day conquers the night.

With each breath, the world wakes,
Awash in hues divine.
In this moment, it takes,
The shape of a grand sign.

Life dances soft and free,
As warmth melts the ice away.
A vibrant symphony,
heralds a brand new day.

Each glisten speaks of hope,
In the light's radiant call.
With each rise, we learn to cope,
As we venture through it all.

Echoes of a Crystalline Dawn

Soft light spills on snowbound fields,
Whispers of night unveil their shields.
A gentle breeze begins to sigh,
As daybreak paints the azure sky.

Frosted branches wear silver lace,
Nature stirs in a tender embrace.
Crystalline moments sparkle bright,
Echoing warmth in morning light.

Birdsongs weave a tender thread,
Above the world where shadows fled.
Each note a promise of new days,
In the dawn's softened, golden rays.

A tapestry of color blooms,
In quiet corners, life resumes.
With every hue, a story told,
In whispers soft, in lights of gold.

Time dances slow upon the glade,
As memories of night do fade.
In echoes, dreams find their way,
To cradle hopes of a brand new day.

Shimmering Frost on Forgotten Paths

The morning's breath brings sparkling frost,
On winding trails, where time was lost.
Each step reveals a crisp delight,
Amongst the trees, draped in white.

Whispers of journeys softly call,
Through icy realms where shadows fall.
Footprints linger, then disappear,
Like fleeting moments, ever near.

Silver glimmers mark the way,
As sunbeams break the cold decay.
A hidden world of wonders grand,
In frozen beauty, hand in hand.

Nature's art, a fleeting scene,
On paths unheard, where few have been.
With every glance, a treasure found,
In shimmering frost that wraps the ground.

Yet time moves on, and soon will glow,
With warmth that melts the silent snow.
But in our hearts these trails remain,
Eternal echoes of joy and pain.

Winter's Palette Whispers

A canvas vast, in muted tones,
Where quiet calm replaces moans.
With every brush of silver lace,
Winter whispers, leaves her trace.

Soft shadows creep through frozen glades,
In timeless dance, the daylight fades.
Each hue a story, rich and deep,
In winter's grip, the earth does sleep.

From midnight blue to paleest gray,
The palette shifts at break of day.
A subtle shift, a breath of air,
Awakens life with tender care.

With each new dawn, fresh colors greet,
In layers thick beneath our feet.
Nature's whispers grace the morn,
As winter's palette is reborn.

Oh, cherish these soft, fleeting days,
Where beauty rests in quiet ways.
Each whisper holds a secret shared,
In winter's heart, we find we dared.

Celestial Frost and First Light

Stars fade softly in the dawn,
As daylight breaks, the night is gone.
Celestial frost on twinkling leaves,
In whispering winds, the world believes.

A tapestry of dreams unfolds,
In sweetened air, the sunrise molds.
The horizon glows, a gentle hue,
As warmth awakens all anew.

Each crystal shard, a whispered prayer,
For fleeting moments, beyond compare.
In silvered light, hope intertwines,
With shadows past, as darkness wanes.

With every ray, a heart ignites,
In shimmering glow of winter's sights.
As day ascends, so too shall we,
Embrace the light, and set it free.

In celestial dance, we find our place,
As dawn extends its warm embrace.
With frost beneath and light above,
In morning's grip, we feel the love.

Serenity in a Shimmering Silence

In the hush of night, stars gleam,
Whispers of peace flow like a dream.
Soft shadows dance on silver tides,
A tranquil heart where stillness abides.

Moonlight weaves through branches bare,
Gently brushing the cool night air.
Calm envelops all within view,
As solitude cradles the world anew.

Rippling waters reflect the sky,
Under the gaze of an owl's eye.
Stillness wraps the earth in its womb,
As night aligns with the silent bloom.

Misty horizons through quiet gaze,
Hope flickers in the fading haze.
In this moment, all things align,
In shimmering silence, I know I'm divine.

Joy drifts softly, like petals fall,
In this refuge, I hear love's call.
Together with twilight, I rest in trance,
Embracing the magic of night's romance.

Light Bends Through Frosted Leaves

Frosted leaves in morning light,
Glimmer softly, pure and bright.
Nature's jewels, frozen lace,
Dancing colors, a warm embrace.

Sunlight filters through the trees,
Shadows quiver with the breeze.
Whispers of warmth in crisp air,
Each moment a gentle prayer.

Glistening paths, where footsteps tread,
Carpeted whispers of winter's thread.
Nature's mirror, bright and clear,
Calling forth the magic near.

In the stillness, beauty thrives,
Every heartbeat, life arrives.
As daylight stretches, shadows slide,
Frosted leaves, where dreams abide.

Together we bask in morning's glow,
Finding peace in the ebb and flow.
Light bends gently, weaving dreams,
In frost-kissed moments, love redeems.

An Arctic Bloom

In the frost where silence reigns,
A brave bloom breaks icy chains.
Petals soft, against the chill,
Defying winter's harshest will.

Colors bold in tundra's embrace,
Nature paints with patient grace.
Amidst the white, a beacon stands,
Hope blooms bright in barren lands.

Each dawn brings a tender sigh,
As sun graces the endless sky.
Gentle warmth on frozen ground,
Life awakens, new joys found.

In frigid nights, stars shine clear,
They hold the whispers of each year.
An Arctic bloom, a tale untold,
Of strength and beauty, fierce and bold.

Resilient heart in icy dew,
In every shade, a story true.
Life finds a way to push through strife,
In quiet defiance, blooms the life.

The Glistening Awakening

Morning breaks with a golden hue,
Nature stirs as night bids adieu.
Soft whispers from leaf to leaf,
Heralding the dawn, beyond belief.

Beneath the sky, rivers gleam,
Mirroring whispers of each dream.
Sparkling dewdrops on blades of grass,
A symphony of light as moments pass.

Mountains cradle the waking light,
Casting shadows that dance in flight.
As the world awakens from sleep,
The promise of joy begins to seep.

A song of colors unfolds wide,
Through the valleys and hillsides.
In every glimmer, hope is found,
As life returns to every sound.

With hearts unburdened, fears eschewed,
We greet the day, with spirits renewed.
In this glistening awakening tale,
Love and light shall always prevail.

Winter's Veil Unfurled

The snowflakes dance on winter's breath,
Blankets soft, a quiet depth.
Trees adorned in white so pure,
Nature's quiet, sweet allure.

Chill winds whisper through the night,
Stars above, a twinkling sight.
Hushed moments, crisp and bright,
In the dream of soft twilight.

Fires crackle, warmth inside,
Hope and joy, our hearts confide.
Frosty air, a crisp delight,
Winter's magic, pure and white.

Footprints trace the path we make,
Silent woods, our hearts awake.
With every step, we find our way,
Together in this winter's play.

As shadows stretch on evening's glow,
Gentle winds begin to blow.
Night wraps us in quiet care,
Winter's veil is woven fair.

Morning's Crystal Embrace

Dewdrops gleam in morning's light,
A canvas painted, fresh and bright.
Birds awaken with songs anew,
In the dawn, the world feels true.

Softly, sunbeams kiss the ground,
Nature stirs, a joyful sound.
Whispers hush the waking trees,
A gentle calm upon the breeze.

Shadows dance as day unfolds,
Every moment, new stories told.
Crystal icicles glisten high,
A brilliance kissed by azure sky.

The air, so crisp, it fills the soul,
In this morn, we're made whole.
Silence reigns, a sacred space,
Enveloped in the sun's warm grace.

With each breath, the world awakes,
A tapestry of life it makes.
In this hour, we find our way,
In morning's crisp, enchanted stay.

Whispers of Icy Light

Moonlight glimmers on frozen streams,
A world transformed, a land of dreams.
Whispers float on chilly air,
As stars above begin to flare.

Trees stand tall in frosty lace,
A silent beauty, a quiet grace.
Footfalls soft on powdered snow,
In this realm, time moves so slow.

Luminous glow, the night inspires,
Hearts ignited like flickering fires.
Each breath visible, a ghostly plume,
Embraced by winter's gentle gloom.

As shadows stretch, horizons fade,
In icy light, memories made.
A world of wonder, pure delight,
In the whispers of the night.

Nature's hush, a secret told,
In the silence, our dreams unfold.
With icy light, our paths align,
In fleeting moments, we intertwine.

When Sunlight Meets the Frost

Morning breaks, a golden hue,
Sunlight dances, fresh and new.
Frosty blades of grass reflect,
Nature's palette, perfect, unchecked.

The warmth of day meets winter's chill,
In this moment, our souls stand still.
Colors burst beneath the sun,
In this realm, we all are one.

With every ray, the shadows flee,
A fleeting touch of warmth and glee.
As melting frost begins to glow,
The earth awakens from its snow.

Across the fields, a shimmer bright,
Nature sings in splendid light.
The world adorned in gold and white,
When sunlight meets the frost at night.

Hand in hand, we walk this way,
In the beauty of the day.
Cherishing each soft caress,
Winter's end, our hearts express.

A Silent Winter's Day

The snow falls soft, a calming veil,
Blanketing the world, where shadows pale.
Trees stand tall, their branches bare,
In the hush of winter's cool, crisp air.

Footprints crunch on pathways white,
While whispers float in the fading light.
A distant crow calls, then flies away,
As silence reigns this winter's day.

Frosty breath, a cloud of dreams,
Nature sleeps, or so it seems.
Underneath, life silently waits,
For the season to open its gates.

In stillness, time stretches slow,
Each moment savored in the snow.
The sun dips low, a golden glow,
A silent winter's day, aglow.

Shining Through the Ice

Icicles hang like crystal spears,
Reflecting light through winter's tears.
Each glinting shard a story tells,
Of frosty nights and gentle bells.

Sunrise spills, a soft embrace,
Melting shadows leave no trace.
In frozen lakes, the colors dance,
Nature's beauty, a fleeting glance.

Pine trees cloaked in sparkling frost,
A world transformed, no beauty lost.
Each droplet caught, like stars at play,
Shining through the ice, come what may.

A whisper of warmth in the air,
Hope springs forth, if we dare.
In the midst of winter's chill,
Shines a light, a promise still.

Whispered Wishes in the Frost

A breath of hope upon the glass,
Whispers travel as moments pass.
Frosted patterns, like lace designs,
Crafting dreams in delicate lines.

The world beneath a shimmering hush,
Carried forward in a gentle rush.
Each wish released into the cold,
Finds its place where stories unfold.

Beneath the stars, the night holds tight,
Embracing secrets in the light.
Silent wishes take their flight,
In the stillness of the night.

Snowflakes twirl, like wishes born,
In the crisp air of early morn.
Each dazzling flake, unique and bright,
Whispered wishes, taking flight.

Threads of Light Upon Snow

Morning breaks with golden rays,
Threads of light on snowy lays.
Nature wakes, adorned in white,
A canvas pure, a wondrous sight.

Sunbeams dance on icy streams,
Carrying hopes and gentle dreams.
Each shimmer brings a soft delight,
Threading warmth into the light.

The world aglow with winter's charm,
A gentle peace, a sweet calm.
Footsteps soft on the frosty ground,
Where joy and beauty can be found.

With every breath, a spark ignites,
A promise held in winter nights.
Each thread of light, a wish to bestow,
Across the land, where white winds blow.

Shimmers in the First Light

The dawn peeks through the trees,
With gold that gently flows,
It dances on the leaves,
Where every shadow glows.

Birds sing a sweet refrain,
Their melodies take flight,
As nature wakes again,
In shimmers of pure light.

The world feels soft and new,
A canvas drawn so wide,
Each color, rich and true,
In morning's gentle tide.

The dew on petals bright,
Like diamonds on display,
Reflecting sheer delight,
As night slips far away.

In this magical hour,
Hope rises with the sun,
Awakening the power,
Of life, it's just begun.

Chilled Radiance of Daybreak

Mist hangs in the cool air,
A blanket softly cast,
Whispers of night still there,
As shadows fade at last.

The sun breaks through the haze,
With fingers warm and bright,
Caressing frozen days,
In chilled radiance, light.

Frost clings to the ground,
Each blade a crystal spark,
A beauty so profound,
In morning's quiet arc.

The horizon blushes pink,
A gentle brush of hue,
Where dreams and thoughts can sink,
As dawn bids night adieu.

Awake, the world breathes deep,
In colors soft and sweet,
While nature starts to leap,
To find the day's heartbeat.

A Palette of Frozen Hues

Snowflakes dance on the breeze,
Creating art divine,
Each flake a masterpiece,
In winter's pure design.

Colors blend on the ground,
Whites, blues, and soft grays,
In silence they abound,
A palette where time plays.

Trees wear coats of ice light,
Their branches hold still dreams,
Reflecting crisp, bright sights,
In winter's softest themes.

Footprints left in the frost,
A story left behind,
Of journeys, paths embossed,
In memories entwined.

As twilight starts to weave,
The stars begin to glow,
An artist's heart believes,
In wonders wrapped in snow.

Shrouded in Silver Silence

The moon hangs high above,
In shadows dim and light,
A tranquil night to love,
In silver's softest sight.

Branches twist and sway,
A whisper in the dark,
As night begins to play,
With every subtle spark.

The world holds its breath still,
Wrapped in a velvet dream,
Where thoughts begin to fill,
In echoes of the stream.

Stars twinkle, secrets shared,
Each one a distant voice,
In this space, souls are bared,
In whispers, they rejoice.

The night, with all its grace,
Enfolds us, heart to heart,
In this serene embrace,
Where every soul's a part.

Reflections on a Glassy Lake

Morning dew on surface clear,
Whispers float in silent cheer,
Mountains cradle skies so bright,
Nature's mirror, pure delight.

Ripples dance, a gentle tease,
A soft breeze brings memories,
Thoughts drift like the clouds above,
In this place I find my love.

Shadows stretch as day awakes,
Awareness in the stillness shakes,
Fleeting moments, time unspun,
In the dawn, I feel as one.

Birds take flight from trees anew,
Echoes of a world askew,
In this space where silence reigns,
A quiet peace, it gently gains.

Glimmers sparkle like a dream,
Life's reflection by the stream,
In this tranquil, sacred nook,
I find solace, and I look.

Illumination in Winter's Frame

Frosty branches, shimmering light,
Blankets white, the earth in sight,
Sunrise paints a golden hue,
Winter's chill, yet warmth is true.

Crystalline sparkles catch the eye,
As snowflakes dance, they drift and fly,
Every breath a cloud of steam,
In this season, I'm a dream.

Footprints trail on frosty ground,
Nature's hush is all around,
In the stillness, hearts will soar,
Seeking winter's hidden lore.

Candles flicker, shadows play,
Evenings draw the light away,
Cocoa warms my tender hands,
As we share our hopes and plans.

In this frame of icy grace,
Love ignites a perfect space,
Together, we will face the chill,
In winter's glow, our hearts will thrill.

Speckles of Sunlit Ice

Sunshine glints on frozen lake,
Each small sparkle seems to wake,
Nature's symphony in bright,
A canvas kissed by morning light.

Children laugh, their voices ring,
Joyful hearts, the warmth they bring,
Gliding softly on the surface,
In this moment, life's the purpose.

Shadows stretch as day unfolds,
Stories whispered, tales retold,
In the shimmer, dreams collide,
With every glide, we take a ride.

Happiness in every breath,
Fragments of the day, like wealth,
On this stage, we dance with grace,
A fleeting, timeless embrace.

As daylight wanes, colors bleed,
In the twilight, hearts take heed,
Under stars, the ice will gleam,
Forever caught within this dream.

Tenderness in a Frosty Morning

Blankets white on morning's face,
Frosted breath in gentle grace,
Softly falling, whispers close,
Nature's beauty, simple prose.

Footprints mark the path we tread,
In this stillness, hopes are bred,
A cup of warmth, hands entwined,
In the chill, our hearts aligned.

Horizon glows with pastel hue,
Brush strokes of a world so new,
Every moment, fresh and bright,
In this morning, pure delight.

Snowflakes dance on winter's breeze,
Quivering leaves on sleeping trees,
In this hush, our spirits rise,
Bound together 'neath the skies.

With each breath of icy air,
Tenderness beyond compare,
In the frosty morning light,
Love will shine, so warm and bright.

Ethereal Glow of Winter Light

Winter whispers soft and low,
A dance of light in flakes of snow.
Moonlit paths, so pure and bright,
Breath of frost in gentle night.

Glistening trees, a silver crown,
Peaceful silence blankets town.
Stars above in shimmering flight,
Embers glow with winter's might.

Each shadow cast, a fleeting glance,
Nature's art, a graceful dance.
Chill that wraps the world so tight,
Holds the dreams of day and night.

In this realm of icy air,
Magic weaves with tender care.
Every blink, a soft delight,
Ethereal glow, in winter's light.

Heartbeats echo, soft and clear,
As the dawn of day draws near.
Hope ignites with morning's sight,
In the warmth of winter light.

Sparkling Horizons

On the edge of dawn's embrace,
Horizon glows with gentle grace.
Streaks of gold in skies so wide,
Awakening the day with pride.

Mountains stand in white-clad dreams,
Beneath the sun, the world redeems.
Rays of warmth, a glimmering sea,
Whispers of what's meant to be.

Flowing rivers, bright and clear,
Mirrored worlds that draw us near.
Endless skies where visions soar,
Sparkling horizons call for more.

Fields of green, in colors bold,
Stories of life, timelessly told.
Nature's palette, rich and bright,
A canvas painted with pure light.

As day unfolds, the magic sings,
Celebration of the joy it brings.
In every glance, in every sight,
Sparkling horizons, pure delight.

The Clarity of a Frozen Day

Morning breaks with icy breath,
Nature still, a dance with death.
Crystal branches, shimmering bright,
The clarity of a frozen sight.

Footprints pressed in glistening snow,
Whispers of winds begin to blow.
Silent woods, a tranquil way,
Wrapped in peace of winter's day.

Frozen lakes reflect the sky,
Every hue a tender sigh.
Sunlight dances on the edge,
Melting hearts along the ledge.

In the stillness, dreams are born,
Promises kept through winter's scorn.
Each breath, a gift, pure and clear,
A frozen day, we hold so dear.

With every glance, a gentle spark,
Illuminating the quiet dark.
Nature's voice, in whispers play,
The clarity of a frozen day.

Shards of Light on a Velvet Blanket

Night descends with velvet grace,
Blanketing the world's embrace.
Stars like shards, so bright and rare,
Twinkling in the tranquil air.

Moonlight spills on fields so wide,
Casting dreams on riverside.
Softly glows the night's delight,
Shards of light, a wondrous sight.

Whispers echo through the trees,
Carried gently on the breeze.
A symphony, both soft and bright,
Illuminates the velvet night.

In stillness lies a tranquil muse,
Awakening with every bruise.
Light that pierces dark's soft shroud,
Shards of hope, both fierce and proud.

As morning beckons, night must fade,
Yet in our hearts, the light's cascades.
Memories of that gentle rite,
Shards of light on a velvet night.

Radiance on a Silver Edge

Moonlight dances on the sea,
Whispers of a night so free.
Stars align in silver streams,
Guiding softly through our dreams.

Waves embrace the sandy shore,
Echoes of the night before.
Each reflection paints the dark,
Kindling bright a hidden spark.

Moments linger in the breeze,
Rustling gently through the trees.
Nature hums a soothing tune,
Beneath the watchful gaze of moon.

Fingers trace the ocean's edge,
Beneath the stars, a loving pledge.
In the light of silver rays,
Hearts entwine in quiet plays.

Radiance wraps the world in glow,
Promises of love we sow.
As dawn breaks with whispered light,
We embrace the coming bright.

The Silence of Frosted Morn

Frosted blades of grass stand tall,
Wrapped in beauty, nature's call.
Morning whispers soft and low,
In the stillness, time moves slow.

Crystals shimmer in the light,
Glimmers soft and pure, so bright.
Every breath a cloud of white,
Painting scenes with sheer delight.

Trees adorned in silver lace,
Silent guardians, they embrace.
Each branch holds a world so still,
Capturing the quiet thrill.

As the sun begins to rise,
Shadows dance beneath the skies.
A soft glow turns frost to dew,
Bringing warmth to all that's new.

Nature holds her breath with grace,
In this peaceful, tender space.
A frosted morn, a gentle sigh,
Whispers of the winter sky.

Glacial Echoes at Sunrise

Mountains stretch in icy might,
Bathed in warmth of morning light.
Echoes whisper through the vale,
   Carried softly on the gale.

Sunrise paints the peaks aglow,
Casting shadows, deep and slow.
Every chime of frozen air,
Sings of beauty, pure and rare.

Rivers carved through ancient ice,
Flowing gently, thought precise.
Nature's art, a frozen dream,
Fractals dance in sunlit gleam.

Glaciers creak, their stories speak,
Of time's passage, strong and sleek.
Each layer holds a tale of old,
Of silent winters, fierce and bold.

As daylight breaks, we stand in awe,
Of the wonders that we draw.
In the stillness, echoes fade,
Beneath the sun, a vast cascade.

Morning's Tapestry of Ice

A quilt of frost upon the ground,
Woven whispers, nature's sound.
Each fragment tells a tale so bright,
Of how the day gives up its night.

Sunbeams thread through icy seams,
Crafting colors, sparking dreams.
Dewdrops glisten, jewels in sight,
Embroidering the world in light.

Trees stand guard, their branches bare,
Crystals hanging, frozen flair.
Every shimmer, every gleam,
Crafts a moment, paints a dream.

Winds of morning softly care,
Stitching warmth in frosty air.
Time unravels with each breath,
In the beauty, life from death.

Amidst the silence, we can find,
A tapestry that binds the mind.
In ice and light, the day begins,
A dance of life, where time spins.

The Awakening of Winter's Palette

Silent snowflakes gently fall,
Covering the world in white,
Brushstrokes of a season's call,
Winter's palette shines so bright.

Trees adorned with icy lace,
Nature's breath, a hush so deep,
Every corner, every space,
In this beauty, we shall steep.

Crystals dance in morning light,
Sparkling like a diamond crown,
The day awakens, pure delight,
As winter wears its velvet gown.

Footprints mark the paths we tread,
Choices made in frosty air,
With every step, our hearts are fed,
Moments captured, slowly shared.

Embrace the chill, let it bind,
In the stillness, magic grows,
Winter whispers in the mind,
A gentle warmth amidst the snows.

A Glacial Call to Day

Whispers ride the icy breeze,
Morning's breath begins to rise,
Glaciers glisten through the trees,
Nature wakes before our eyes.

Sunlight breaks the frosty veil,
Casting shadows on the ground,
In this beauty, hearts exhale,
Dancing softly, all around.

Each breath forms a crystal plume,
Frosty patterns in the air,
Where the world begins to bloom,
In shared glances, we declare.

Moments linger, still and clear,
A glacial call awakens time,
As day unfolds, we draw near,
Finding rhythm, life's perfect rhyme.

Together in this winter's grace,
We gather warmth in every glance,
In the calm, we find our place,
In glacial calls, we sway, we dance.

Tranquil Whispers of Ice

Tranquility in every flake,
Gentle whispers in the night,
Ice transforms the world we make,
Silver reflections, purest light.

Silence drapes like velvet cloth,
Crystals sparkle, dreams take flight,
In the stillness, find the broth,
Of winter's peace, so warm and bright.

Footsteps echo on the ground,
With each crunch, a story told,
In the hush, a magic found,
Nature's beauty, soft and bold.

Winter paints with icy hands,
Crafting visions, wild and free,
Every edge and line expands,
In tranquil whispers, we shall see.

As the night descends again,
Stars alight in frozen sky,
In this realm where dreams begin,
Whispers of ice shall never die.

Celestial Chill of First Light

In the dawn, a chill descends,
Celestial hues awaken slow,
Colors blend as daylight bends,
A tapestry of frost and glow.

Morning whispers, crisp and clear,
Nature stretches with a sigh,
In this moment, hold it near,
As sun and frost become the sky.

Starlit remnants fade away,
Casting shadows on the snow,
In this dance of night and day,
Winter's beauty starts to show.

Every breath a misty plume,
Painting stories in the air,
A world cloaked in silent gloom,
Turns to light, a warming glare.

With each ray, the chill retreats,
Hope ignites in amber bright,
Winter leaves us with soft beats,
Celestial chill of first light.

A Glimmering Start

In the hush of dawn's embrace,
Light dances on the dew-kissed lace.
Soft whispers of the day begin,
A world anew, fresh hopes within.

Birds serenade the waking sky,
With melodies that gently fly.
Golden rays break through the night,
Promising warmth, a pure delight.

Each moment holds a gentle spark,
Moments glimmer, bright and stark.
Embrace the day with open heart,
In every breath, a brand new start.

The flowers bloom, the colors blend,
Nature's canvas, there to tend.
As shadows fade and dreams ignite,
A glimmering start, pure and bright.

Take a step into the light,
Feel the joy, let spirits bright.
With every dawn, fresh paths appear,
Together ignite, cast away fear.

Winter's Breath on the Horizon

A chill descends upon the ground,
Whispers of winter all around.
Frosty air paints trees with grace,
Nature dons her white embrace.

The breath of ice, so crisp and clear,
Winds carry tales that we hold dear.
Fields asleep in blankets, white,
Dreaming softly through the night.

Icicles gleam like jewels bright,
In the stillness, pure delight.
Footsteps crunch on fading trails,
Silence tells of winter's tales.

A distant sunset casts a glow,
Reflecting shades of softest snow.
The horizon's edge, a tranquil sight,
Winter's breath, both cold and light.

As fires crackle, hearts unite,
Sharing warmth through snowy nights.
In every flake, a story told,
Winter's peace in heart and soul.

Hypnotic Gleam of Daylight

The sun ascends with radiant beams,
Awakening the world's soft dreams.
Golden light in every space,
A hypnotic dance, a warm embrace.

Clouds drift lazily on high,
Casting shadows as they sigh.
Fields awaken, colors burst,
In daylight's gleam, we quench our thirst.

Every ray, a gentle touch,
Filling hearts, we crave so much.
Nature hums in vibrant hue,
With the light, our spirits renew.

As the day unfolds its grace,
Each moment finds its rightful place.
In sunlight's glow, we feel alive,
In this gleam, our dreams can thrive.

Let's chase the light, embrace the day,
With open hearts, we find our way.
The hypnotic gleam, a guiding star,
In every journey, near or far.

Frosty Mornings Whisper Secrets

Underneath the morning mist,
Frosty whispers can't resist.
Nature speaks in silent tones,
A world adorned in icy bones.

The air is crisp, sensations keen,
Trees wear coats of shimmering sheen.
Each breath forms a misty cloud,
Wrapped in silence, calm and proud.

Footsteps softly crunch the frost,
Every moment feels like lost.
Whispers from the earth below,
Secrets in the chill bestow.

Birds appear, their songs so clear,
Life awakens, free of fear.
Frosty mornings, magic real,
In the quiet, hearts can heal.

As sunlight breaks the chilly spell,
Warmth returns, we know it well.
With every secret that we keep,
Frosty mornings, dreams run deep.

Dawn's Breath on Polished Earth

A whisper soft, the dawn does creep,
Painting the sky where shadows sleep.
The dew awakens, glistening bright,
As day unfurls, embracing light.

Birds take wing, in flight so free,
Each note they sing, a melody.
The world stirs slowly, with tender grace,
In golden hues, the night we chase.

The trees awaken, their branches sway,
In morning's glow, they greet the day.
The earth, refreshed, breathes in the sun,
In this new dawn, our hearts are one.

Fields of green, kissed by the sun,
The colors blend, a day begun.
Every moment, a treasure found,
In dawn's embrace, we are unbound.

With every step, we walk anew,
In the light of day, our spirits grew.
Dawn's breath sweet, upon the earth,
A symphony of joy and mirth.

Glittering Secrets of Dawn

In the stillness, secrets lie,
Twinkling softly in the sky.
Morning whispers, tales unfold,
Of sparkling dreams from nights of old.

Each ray of light begins to weave,
A tapestry that we believe.
Glittering gems on leaves so bright,
Guiding us to the warmth of light.

The sun arises, bold and true,
Painting horizons in vibrant hue.
With every moment, magic's born,
In glittering dawn, a world reborn.

Nature joins in the joyful song,
As shadows fade, we all belong.
The secrets shared, the stories told,
In every heart, the dawn unfolds.

So let us dance in morning's grace,
Embracing love in this special place.
Together here, we find our way,
In glittering secrets of the day.

Frost-kissed Bloom

In silent gardens, wonders grow,
Where frosty whispers gently blow.
Petals shimmer with icy breath,
A fragile beauty, hint of death.

Beneath the frost, life still persists,
Each bud a promise, nature's tryst.
In wintry light, they dance and sway,
A testament to warmer days.

The sun peeks in, a golden ray,
Melted crystals drift away.
Frost-kissed blooms, a sight so rare,
Reveal the spring that's hidden there.

With every dawn, the cycle turns,
A lesson in the heart that yearns.
Though winter clings, hope does not fade,
In nature's hands, a grand charade.

So let us cherish every phase,
For life anew in myriad ways.
Frost-kissed blooms, we hold them dear,
A transient gift, forever near.

Light Breaking Through the Frost

When darkness wanes, the light appears,
Breaking through, it calms our fears.
The frosty veil begins to lift,
In tender warmth, we find our gift.

Sunbeams dance on sparkling ground,
In gentle whispers, hope is found.
As shadows vanish, colors bloom,
From icy nights, we rise from gloom.

The world awakens, fresh and new,
In golden shades, a vibrant view.
Light breaking through, a sweet embrace,
Filling our hearts with warmth and grace.

Every crystal, every gleam,
Fashions life into a dream.
A moment's breath, soft and pure,
In nature's arms, we find our cure.

So let the light lead us each day,
Through winding paths, come what may.
For in the frost, life takes its cue,
And with each dawn, we are renewed.

A Symphony in White

Snowflakes dance upon the breeze,
A blanket soft, the world at ease.
Whispers of winter gently call,
In this serene, enchanted hall.

Icicles hang, a crystal bright,
Reflections shimmer in pure white.
Nature's chorus, sweet and clear,
The silent song we long to hear.

Fields of frost, a glistening sheet,
Traces of magic beneath our feet.
Each branch adorned in soft embrace,
A vision of pure, enchanting grace.

The moonlight paints the night so still,
Enchanting views upon the hill.
With every breath, the cold so pure,
In winter's symphony, we endure.

So let us wander through the night,
Bathed in a softly glowing light.
In the embrace of winter's care,
A symphony may linger there.

Dawn's Glittering Secrets

In the east, the sun ignites,
Casting dreams on tranquil nights.
Gold and pink begin to blend,
Heralding the day's ascent.

Morning dew like diamonds gleam,
Nature wakes from tranquil dream.
Fingers of light stretch and grow,
Painting landscapes, soft aglow.

Whispers in the gentle air,
Secrets held in sunlight's stare.
Birds begin their morning songs,
Echoes where the heart belongs.

Colors splash in vibrant hues,
Each dawn brings a world anew.
Shadows fade, the night withdraws,
In this dance, life gives applause.

So let us cherish golden rays,
As the world in wonder sways.
Dawn's embrace, a fleeting kiss,
Awakens us to morning bliss.

Pale Light Through a Frozen Lens

In a world enshrined in ice,
Pale light falls, so soft and nice.
Shadows linger, whispers fleet,
Frozen tales our hearts repeat.

Glistening paths of silver trails,
Eerie echoes, distant wails.
Through the frost, a sight divine,
Nature's beauty, pure and fine.

Branches crack with quiet grace,
The stillness holds a solemn place.
Veils of white, the earth adorns,
In this realm where silence mourns.

Cold breaths swirl in frosty air,
In their embrace, we find despair.
Yet within this frozen scene,
Life's resilience can be seen.

So stand still, let your heart reflect,
On the beauty life connects.
Through the lens of winter's night,
We find warmth in pale moonlight.

Awakening the Slumbering Frost

Winter's breath begins to fade,
As spring unfurls, a gentle braid.
From under snow, the earth awakes,
Life emerges in small mistakes.

Buds break free from icy chains,
Color splashes through the lanes.
Softly chirps a distant bird,
In this calm, the world is stirred.

Sunlight breaks with tender grace,
Melting frost from every place.
Glistening drops like jewels fall,
Nature's laughter, a beckoning call.

Fields once white, now green and bright,
Whispers of the coming light.
Each soft breeze a love song knows,
In the bloom, true beauty grows.

So let us dance with joy restored,
As life awakens, love adored.
Through every heart, a spark does rise,
Awakening the world with skies.

The Whispering Hues of Early Light

The dawn unfolds with gentle grace,
Soft colors spill across the space.
A palette bright, yet calm and sweet,
As day breaks forth, the night retreat.

Birds chirp softly in the trees,
Carried by the delicate breeze.
Golden warmth begins to rise,
Painting dreams across the skies.

Each hue whispers a secret tale,
Of morning's breath, the night's exhale.
A canvas vast, forever wide,
In this moment, shadows hide.

With every stroke, the colors blend,
As night gives way, the day's ascend.
The whispering hues, a sweet embrace,
Awakening the world with grace.

In tranquil silence, hearts ignite,
Beneath the whispering early light.
Hope rises with the sun's ascent,
In every hue, the day is spent.

Light's Dance on the Frost

Morning glimmers on the frost,
Each whispering ray, a beauty lost.
Crystals shimmer in retreat,
As dawn paints all beneath its feet.

A ballet of warmth on icy ground,
Nature's silence, a soothing sound.
Silver sparkles twirl and sway,
In the gentle light of day.

Footsteps crunch, a rhythmic beat,
While shadows play where cold winds meet.
Beneath the sun's embrace and cheer,
The frost awakens, crystal clear.

Every glint, a fleeting kiss,
A moment caught in winter's bliss.
Here, the world is stark but bright,
In the dance of morning light.

As shadows lengthen, day grows bold,
Yet in this dance, pure magic unfolds.
With each soft glow, the frost turns gold,
In light's embrace, we find our hold.

Sunlight Breaking the Ice

Cracks form gently on the glass,
Sunlight breaks, the moments pass.
Winter's grip begins to yield,
As warmth awakens the frozen field.

Reflecting rays upon the lake,
Softly whispering, hearts awake.
The ice, a canvas of silver hue,
Transforming into skies so blue.

With every beam that graces the shore,
Nature sighs and asks for more.
In this dance of light and freeze,
Life emerges with gentle ease.

Ripples form where silence stood,
In sunlight's touch, the world feels good.
Promises linger in the warm embrace,
As winter's chill begins to erase.

Sunlight's laughter paints the air,
With golden tones everywhere.
Ice retreats with every ray,
In this moment, winter gives way.

Subtle Glow of a Wintry World

In twilight's hush, a glow appears,
Whispers softly through the years.
Snowflakes dance in gentle flight,
A subtle glow, the world feels right.

Moonlight bathes the frozen scene,
Casting silver where once was green.
Branches glisten, a fragile lace,
In this wintry trance, a warm embrace.

Every shimmer tells a tale,
Of secrets held in winter's veil.
Soft breaths linger in the air,
A tranquil moment, sweet and rare.

Underneath the starlit sky,
Dreams unfold as night drifts by.
With each flutter of the snow,
The subtle glow begins to flow.

As time slows down, fears take flight,
Wrapped in warmth of winter's light.
The world transforms in night's still hold,
In the subtle glow, pure and bold.

Winter's Awakening in Light

Soft whispers float on the air,
Sunlight dances, a gentle glare.
Snowflakes shimmer, pure and bright,
Nature stirs in morning light.

Branches droop, adorned in white,
Crystals glisten, a wondrous sight.
The world reborn, a calm delight,
Winter breathes, the heart takes flight.

Footprints trace a silent path,
Echoes of a snowy wrath.
In this hush, new dreams ignite,
Life awakens, hearts feel light.

Frozen ponds mirror the skies,
Underneath, the stillness lies.
Every inhale brings a chill,
Yet warmth blooms against the thrill.

Veils of fog gently unwind,
As the dawn lets go, unconfined.
Tender hues of pink and gold,
Awakening stories yet untold.

Enchanted by the Crystal Morning

Morning breaks with silent grace,
Crystals glint in their embrace.
Nature whispers, soft and kind,
In this magic, peace we find.

Each twinkle holds a hidden dream,
Sunbeams weave an icy seam.
Trees stand tall, a frozen choir,
As the world breathes, wrapped in fire.

Rivers flow beneath the frost,
Beauty found, yet never lost.
Every branch an artful frame,
In this wonder, all the same.

Birds awaken, serenade,
Their songs burst forth, unafraid.
In the stillness, time stands still,
Magic dances, hearts to fill.

Glistening paths through untouched snow,
Where dreams wander, wild and slow.
In this realm, our spirits soar,
Enchanted mornings, evermore.

A Symphony of Frosted Light

Wind chimes whisper in the breeze,
Nature's song brings hearts to ease.
Each flake a note in winter's rhyme,
Telling tales of distant time.

Footprints crunch on paths of white,
Echoes of the day's first light.
A canvas brushed with silver hues,
In this symphony, we choose.

Icy tendrils wrap around,
A winter's hush, a tranquil sound.
With every breath, the chill excites,
Bringing forth the frosted sights.

Sunrise paints the world anew,
Golden rays break through the blue.
Awakening the sleepy ground,
Where beauty's essence can be found.

Harmony in every sight,
Winter's magic, pure delight.
Together, hearts sing in tune,
With a promise of the moon.

Radiant Reflections of a Chilled Dawn

Dawn ascends with hues of rose,
A chilling breath, the day bestows.
Mirrored lakes, a canvas pure,
Reflections dance, warm and sure.

Frost-kissed grasses gently sway,
As sunlight spills upon the day.
Each spark a memory, bright and bold,
Tales of warmth in winter's cold.

Gentle sighs through whispering pines,
Nature's heart in perfect lines.
Every shadow, every light,
Crafts a story, day and night.

Branches brush the glowing sky,
As time flows, a soft goodbye.
Step by step, the world unfolds,
Radiant truths in glimmers told.

With each breath, the magic deep,
In winter's arms, treasures we keep.
A chill that wraps, yet fills with grace,
Radiant moments, warm embrace.

Serenade of the Winter Sunrise

In whispers soft, the day begins,
Melting frost, where silence thins.
Golden rays through branches peek,
Nature's breath, serene and meek.

The icy crystals catch the light,
A tapestry so pure and bright.
Every flake, a work of art,
Winter's canvas, a brand new start.

The world adorned in glistening white,
Birds take flight in morning's sight.
A melody in the crisp, still air,
Serenade of winter, beyond compare.

With each step, the crunching sound,
Echoes softly, all around.
In this beauty, hearts align,
Winter's song, a sweet design.

As shadows fade, warmth follows near,
A promise whispered, the spring is here.
But in this moment, let us stay,
To cherish winter's bright display.

Frosted Dreams Unveiled

Beneath the blanket, calm and deep,
Lies a world in winter's keep.
Frosted dreams begin to stir,
Nature's hush, a gentle purr.

Each branch adorned with icy lace,
Time pauses, embraces grace.
Crystal whispers in the air,
Fragrant pine, a sign we care.

Echoes of the night retreat,
Mornings wrapped in warmth compete.
The sun arrives, a golden beam,
Awakening our frosted dream.

Footprints trace through fields of white,
A dance beneath the morning light.
In this realm, our worries cease,
Frosted dreams, a moment's peace.

As daylight spreads across the land,
We hold the beauty close at hand.
For with each thaw, new hope unfurls,
In winter's enchantment, time swirls.

Luminous Chill of Early Light

The dawn awakens with a chill,
Painting skies with light, so still.
Shadows dance on crisp white ground,
In silence, warmth will soon abound.

Mist rises like a gentle sigh,
Underneath the cobalt sky.
Birdsong fills the frosty air,
A symphony, both bright and rare.

Each breath visible, a fleeting cloud,
Nature wakes, beneath its shroud.
The sun ignites the frozen scene,
A vibrant world, replete, serene.

Step by step through trees so bare,
The chill entwines with tender care.
A journey starts as daylight calls,
Embracing beauty, winter sprawls.

With every ray that pierces through,
Hope blooms fresh, as with each hue.
In this moment, hold on tight,
To the luminous chill of early light.

A Frosty Symphony of Colors

In silence, snowflakes gently fall,
A frosty symphony, nature's call.
Colors mingle, white and blue,
In this world, every hue.

Twilight whispers, day's farewell,
Underneath a frosted spell.
Trees wear coats of shimmering frost,
In this quiet, we count our cost.

Icicles dangle, sharp and clear,
Reflecting joys, fleeting cheer.
The landscape glows in twilight's grace,
A canvas crafted, time can't erase.

Carried on the winter breeze,
Echoes of laughter through the trees.
Children's dreams on sleds take flight,
In every heart, pure delight.

As darkness falls, the stars ignite,
In the stillness, a soothing night.
A frosty symphony, our hearts unfold,
In winter's arms, a story told.

A Glimmering Awakening

In the hush of dawn's first light,
A world emerges, calm and bright.
Golden rays through branches weave,
Whispers of the day, we believe.

Softly stirs the sleeping earth,
Each moment holds a tender worth.
Tales of dreams begin to flow,
As life awakens, time's sweet show.

Colors dance on morning's breeze,
Nature sings with joyful ease.
Glimmers touch the dewdrop's face,
A symphony in nature's grace.

Clouds part ways, the sun ascends,
In harmony, the day descends.
With each breath, a chance renewed,
In this light, our hopes are brewed.

Take a step into the glow,
Let the beauty overflow.
For in this dawn, we find our place,
In the warmth of time's embrace.

Chilled Hues of Awakening

Frosted breath upon the morn,
A gentle chill where dreams are born.
Pastel skies in muted tone,
Whispers soft, yet all alone.

Shadows linger, long and deep,
Secrets that the night will keep.
Each hue glows with a frozen heart,
In shades of gray, the world does start.

Icicles hang, a crystal din,
Nature's stillness tucked within.
Silent echoes softly call,
Awakening as night does fall.

In quiet moments, hope ignites,
Chilled hues come to gather sights.
The sun peeks through with timid grace,
Inviting warmth to take its place.

As colors merge in soft embrace,
The chill gives way to a bright space.
With every breath, the world awakes,
In frozen dreams, our spirit breaks.

Dreams Wrapped in Ice

In the cradle of the night,
Dreams like whispers take their flight.
Wrapped in frost, they softly gleam,
Chasing echoes of a dream.

Frigid winds, a haunting tune,
Lullabies beneath the moon.
Silent wishes float and glide,
Within the ice, our hopes abide.

Each thought encased, a fragile spark,
In winter's hands, they leave a mark.
Twinkling visions, pure and bright,
In frozen realms, we'll find our light.

Through the cold, desire flows,
In the stillness, passion grows.
For in this ice, we learn to trust,
That dreams can thaw, as dreams we must.

As dawn descends on silver dreams,
Unlocking paths with radiant beams.
Fractured ice, a tale to share,
In the warmth of love, we dare.

Glacial Threads of Dawn

Beneath the veil of icy skies,
Glacial threads, a soft surprise.
Stitching moments, light and cold,
In the dawn, new stories told.

Fingers of frost weave through the morn,
Creating patterns fresh and worn.
Each warmth a thread, gently spun,
In the cradle of the rising sun.

Threads of light begin to break,
Colors merge, awake, awake!
Nature's loom, a vibrant race,
Weaving joy in every space.

With tender gaze, the world observes,
Glacial beauty, calm reserves.
In each whisper, life unfolds,
Through the dawn, the magic molds.

So let the threads of day entwine,
In heart and spirit, we shall shine.
As dawn unfurls its fabric grand,
We find our dreams in morning's hand.

Glowing Frost Kisses the World

In the dawn's soft light, it glistens bright,
A silver touch on every sight,
Whispers of winter, so pure, so bold,
A tapestry of dreams, spun from cold.

Trees wear crystals, a shimmering dress,
Each branch adorned, nature's caress,
Soft whispers echo through the still air,
As the world awakens, lost in a stare.

Rivers sigh beneath a frosty glaze,
Reflecting sunlight in a dainty haze,
Footprints crunch on pathways of white,
In this frozen wonder, hearts take flight.

The sky blushes in hues of pale pink,
Inviting thoughts that make us think,
Each breath a cloud, dancing on air,
In glowing frost, we find our share.

As shadows stretch and day turns to night,
The moon rises, casting gentle light,
Glowing frost, our world at rest,
In winter's arms, we are truly blessed.

Serenity in a Winter's Cradle

Snowflakes drift with tender grace,
A quiet hush in every space,
Blankets white cover the ground,
In winter's cradle, peace is found.

Trees stand still, as if to dream,
Holding secrets of a frozen theme,
Nature pauses, time takes a breath,
In this silence, there's beauty in death.

A gentle breeze weaves through the pines,
Whispering softly, where the heart aligns,
In this stillness, worries fade away,
Bathed in serenity, we gently sway.

Icicles hang like crystal tears,
Capturing moments of fleeting years,
Each glimmer reflects a frozen smile,
Inviting us to linger awhile.

As the sun dips low, the glow ignites,
Painting the sky with amber lights,
In winter's embrace, we find our peace,
A cradle of calm, where all fears cease.

The Promise of Chilled Light

Morning breaks with a tender gleam,
Frost covers fields, a whispered dream,
Promises linger in every flake,
Bringing hope through the chill we take.

Shadows dance as the sun climbs high,
Casting warmth in an azure sky,
Frosted whispers in a vibrant hue,
A promise of light, forever new.

Every corner holds a spark of joy,
Even silence feels like a toy,
Laughter echoes in the crisp air,
In this kingdom of frost, we share.

With every step, we tread in delight,
Feeling the magic of chilled light,
Crisp and clear, it calls our name,
In the heart of winter, nothing's the same.

As twilight falls and the chill expands,
Stars twinkle brightly, a dance in bands,
The promise of winter, steadfast and bright,
Fills our souls with an endless light.

A Dance Across Frosted Meadows

Frosted meadows, a blanket so wide,
Where dreams are spun and spirits abide,
Each blade of grass, a jeweled affair,
In the dance of winter, we find our share.

Footsteps crunch on a powdery stage,
The world adorned, a peaceful page,
Snowflakes twirl like delicate sprites,
In the glow of day, as joy ignites.

Clouds float gently, a soft embrace,
Wrap the earth in a serene trace,
Sunlight kisses the frosty ground,
In this splendid beauty, love is found.

Gentle breezes weave through the scene,
Nature's rhythm, a song so keen,
In every rustle, the whispers blend,
A dance across meadows, where hearts mend.

As twilight falls, the stars appear,
A shimmering dance, so bright and clear,
In the evening's hush, we pause and sway,
Frosted meadows hold our hearts at play.

Diamonds Upon the Frozen Lake

Upon the ice, they shimmer bright,
Like scattered stars in the night.
A crystal dance, a silent song,
Nature's grace where dreams belong.

Whispers of winter fill the air,
Each frozen gem, a jewel rare.
As shadows stretch, the sun dips low,
Transforming white to rosy glow.

Footsteps trace the calm expanse,
Life's fleeting moments in a glance.
With every breath, a story unfolds,
In the chill, warmth lies untold.

Reflections mirror life so true,
In this world of frosty hue.
The lake holds secrets, deep and wide,
A tranquil hope where dreams reside.

As night descends, the scene transforms,
The lake reflects what beauty warms.
In this stillness, hearts ignite,
Diamonds shine, embracing light.

A New Day Wrapped in Chill

Morning breaks with gentle sigh,
Amidst the frost, the earth does lie.
A blanket white on fields so wide,
Nature's quilt, where dreams abide.

Soft breezes whisper through the trees,
Carrying whispers of gentle freeze.
The sun peeks through, a golden ray,
A promise new, a brand new day.

With every breath, the stillness grows,
As frost-kissed petals wear winter's clothes.
Eager buds await the sun's warm kiss,
In this chill, there's hidden bliss.

Birds take flight in the azure sky,
A dance of freedom, soaring high.
Each flutter sings of life anew,
Wrapped in moments, pure and true.

In the quiet of each morning light,
Hope awakens, free from night.
A new day dawns, both fresh and bright,
Filled with promise, love, and light.

Glacial Hues Beneath Rising Stars

Stars emerge in the velvet night,
A tapestry of brilliant light.
Glacial hues shimmer, soft and clear,
Reflecting dreams both far and near.

The mountains stand, so bold, so high,
Beneath a canopy of sky.
Each peak adorned with night's embrace,
A silent vigil over this space.

Ice flows gently, a whispering stream,
Carving pathways, a frozen dream.
The nightingale sings its elusive tune,
Under the watch of the sparkling moon.

Time pauses here, in the frozen deep,
Awakening wonders that softly creep.
Where shadows dance and secrets gleam,
Glacial hues tell tales that beam.

As dawn approaches, the stars will fade,
Yet memories linger, never betrayed.
In the heart of night, where silence reigns,
The beauty of stars forever remains.

The Beauty of Frost-Kissed Morn

Frost-kissed petals greet the dawn,
A gentle sigh, the night now gone.
Nature wakes in a tranquil trance,
Inviting all to join the dance.

Each blade of grass glimmers anew,
Enveloped in a shimmering dew.
The world transformed in icy lace,
A moment captured, pure embrace.

Sunlight filters through the trees,
A cascade of warmth, a tender breeze.
Birdsongs rise as shadows flee,
In this morn, life dances free.

Golden rays stretch wide and far,
Touching earth with a velvet spar.
The beauty blooms where frost has tread,
Awakening dreams that gently spread.

As daylight breaks, the world ignites,
With colors bold, enchanting sights.
Frost-kissed morn, a gift divine,
Whispers of joy in every line.